Kids Laugh Ch

Would You Rather?

Easter Edition

Hilarious Questions, Silly Choices, and
Wacky Scenarios

JOYLAND

Kids Laugh Challenge Bonus Play

Join our special Facebook Group at
Joyland For Kids
or
send an email to:
Joylandforkids@gmail.com
and you will get the following

- ❤ Bonus Would You Rather questions
- ❤ An Entry in Our Monthly Giveaway of $25 Amazon Gift card!
- ❤ Early Access to new books

We draw a new winner each month and will contact you via email or the facebook group.

Good Luck!

Kids Laugh Challenge

Would You Rather?

Easter Edition

How do you play?

The Would You Rather Challenge consists of 10 rounds with 1 tie-breaker round at the end. At least 2 players are needed to play this game. Face your opponent and decide who is "**Easter Egg 1**" and who is "**Easter Egg 2**". If you have 3 or 4 players, you can decide who belongs to **Easter Egg Group 1** and **Easter Egg Group 2**. The goal of the game is to score points by make the other players laugh.

After completing each round, tally up the point and whoever gets the most points is the **Round Champion**. Add all the points from the 10 round to see who is **the Laugh Champion**. If the score is a tie after round 10, go for the tie-breaker round 11 where the Winner takes all.

What are the rules?
Easter Egg 1 starts first. Read the questions aloud and choose an answer. The same player will then explain why they chose that answer in the funniest and silliest way possible. If the explanation makes "**Easter Egg 2**"laugh, then "**Easter Egg 1**" scores a point. Take turns going back and forth and write down the score at the end of each round.

How do you get started?
Flip a coin. The Easter Egg that guesses it correctly starts first.

BONUS TIP: Making funny voices, silly dance moves or wacky facial expressions will make your opponent laugh!

Most Importantly: Remember to have fun and enjoy the game!

Note: The scenarios listed in the book are solely for fun and games!Please do NOT attempt any scenarios at home!

ROUND

1

Easter Egg 1

Would you rather have to hop like a bunny OR have to crawl like a caterpillar to school everyday?

Funny Point____/1

Would you rather it rain marshmallows OR it rain jellybeans on the first day of spring?

Funny Point____/1

Easter Egg 1

Would you rather have an Easter egg for a nose OR have two Easter eggs for eyes?

Funny Point____/1

Would you rather have to wear a shirt made out of flowers OR have to wear a shirt made out of bird's feathers on the first day of summer?

Funny Point____/1

11

Easter Egg 1

Would you rather eat carrots dipped in chocolate or drink a chocolate carrot smoothie?

Funny Point____/1

Would you rather wear a hat that looks like a bunny's head OR wear a hat that looks like a big tree?

Funny Point____/1

STOP: Now pass the book to Easter Egg 2

Easter Egg 2

Remember to Explain Your Answer

Would you rather open up a lemonade stand OR host an Easter play in front of the whole neighborhood on the first day of spring?

Funny Point____/1

Would you rather have hair with the colors of the rainbow OR have a bunny nose?

Funny Point____/1

Easter Egg 2

Would you rather dance around in the rain or sleep on the clouds?

Funny Point____/1

Would you rather it was really windy OR it was really cloudy on the first day of spring?

Funny Point____/1

Easter Egg 2

Remember to Explain Your Answer

Would you rather eat all of your Easter eggs in one day OR not have any Easter eggs at all?

Funny Point____/1

Would you rather search for 100 Easter eggs and half of them have money in them OR search for 500 Easter eggs and all of the eggs have money in them but you only have 10 minutes to find them all?

Funny Point____/1

🥕 Easter Egg 1

_____/6

Round 1 Total Score

🥕 Easter Egg 2

_____/6

Round 1 Total Score

ROUND

2

Easter Egg 1

Remember to Explain Your Answer

Would you rather have the walls of your bedroom be covered in painted Easter eggs OR have the walls of your bedroom be covered in painted Easter bunnies?

Funny Point____/1

Would you rather slide down a rainbow OR jump on the clouds like a trampoline?

Funny Point____/1

Easter Egg 1

Remember to Explain Your Answer

Would you rather turn into a ladybug OR turn into a butterfly on the first day of spring?

Funny Point____/1

Would you rather drink a glass of milk while eating your chocolate OR drink a cup of tea while eating your chocolate?

Funny Point____/1

Easter Egg 1

Would you rather spend all of Spring off from school OR spend all of winter off from school?

Funny Point____/1

Would you rather read a book about bunnies trying to hide chocolate eggs in time for Easter OR watch a movie about talking flowers?

Funny Point____/1

STOP: Now pass the book to Easter Egg 2

Easter Egg 2

Would you rather play a game of hide and seek outside in the rain OR inside a small house?

Funny Point____/1

Would you rather paint your face to look like an Easter egg OR wear fake bunny ears and fake bunny teeth for a whole week?

Funny Point____/1

Easter Egg 1

Remember to Explain Your Answer

Would you rather play a video game of a chicken painting Easter eggs OR of a bunny hiding the Easter eggs?

Funny Point____/1

Would you rather swim in the middle of a thunderstorm OR go for a long walk on a hot sunny day?

Funny Point____/1

Easter Egg 1

Remember to Explain Your Answer

Would you rather have hot-cross buns for breakfast OR waffles with ice-cream for breakfast?

Funny Point____/1

Would you rather have to solve riddles to find all of your Easter eggs OR have to follow a long and complicated map?

Funny Point____/1

Easter Egg 1

_____/6

Round 2 Total Score

Easter Egg 2

_____/6

Round 2 Total Score

ROUND

3

Easter Egg 1

Would you rather do a cannon-ball jump into an ice-cold lake OR soak your hair in chocolate?

Funny Point____/1

Would you rather decorate your room's walls with all kinds of spring flowers OR decorate your room's ceiling with a bunch of glow in the dark stars and a big moon?

Funny Point____/1

Easter Egg 1

Remember to Explain Your Answer

Would you rather be able to fly like a bird OR grow really tall like a tree?

Funny Point____/1

Would you rather have an Easter Egg fight OR have a water balloon fight?

Funny Point____/1

Easter Egg 1

Would you rather have a garden full of flowers that look ugly but smell great OR have a garden full of flowers that look beautiful but smell disgusting?

Funny Point____/1

Would you rather be stuck inside a candy shop because of a rainstorm on the first day of Spring OR be stuck inside a pet shop where the pets are allowed to run around freely?

Funny Point____/1

Easter Egg 2

Remember to Explain Your Answer

Would you rather travel to an island on an old rowing boat OR have to walk all the way on an old rickety, wooden bridge?

Funny Point____/1

Would you rather have a pet bunny that can play the drums really well OR have a pet bunny that can play video games really well?

Funny Point____/1

Easter Egg 2

Remember to Explain Your Answer

Would you rather be covered from head to toe in bunny fur OR be covered from head to toe with chicken feathers?

Funny Point____/1

Would you rather spend Easter at home with all of your friends and family playing games, and eating chocolate OR spend Easter on vacation in whatever country you want but you're by yourself with only Easter eggs?

Funny Point____/1

Easter Egg 2

Remember to Explain Your Answer

Would you rather have every day be Easter day or have every day be your birthday?

Funny Point____/1

Would you rather the Easter Bunny bring you a chocolate egg every day of the year OR have Santa Claus bring you a small present every day of the year?

Funny Point____/1

🥕 Easter Egg 1

_____/6

Round 3 Total Score

🥕 Easter Egg 2

_____/6

Round 3 Total Score

ROUND

4

Easter Egg 1

Would you rather find a hundred small chocolate eggs on Easter morning OR find one chocolate egg the size of a car on Easter morning?

Funny Point____/1

Would you rather have to spring clean your room every day of spring OR spring clean your whole house including the garden just one day in spring?

Funny Point____/1

Easter Egg 1

Remember to Explain Your Answer

Would you rather it be really bright and sunny OR it be really cold and foggy on the first day of spring?

Funny Point____/1

Would you rather be at school on Easter day but then get the rest of spring off from school OR get Easter day off from school but have to go to school for the rest of spring?

Funny Point____/1

Easter Egg 1

Would you rather get as many chocolate eggs as you want on Easter day OR get all of the toys you want on Christmas day?

Funny Point____/1

Would you rather be gifted a newborn puppy that can talk on the OR be gifted a newborn kitten that can dance?

Funny Point____/1

STOP: Now pass the book to Easter Egg 2

Easter Egg 2

Remember to Explain Your Answer

Would you rather be able to make it rain OR be able to make it snow whenever you want?

Funny Point____/1

Would you rather have Easter day land on any day you want it to each year OR have it land on a random day each year?

Funny Point____/1

Easter Egg 1

Would you rather help the Easter Bunny make his chocolate eggs OR hide his chocolate eggs?

Funny Point____/1

Would you rather have a seed in a flower pot that is ready to grow into a big and tall flower OR have someone pick a fully grown flower and put it in a vase for you?

Funny Point____/1

38

Easter Egg 1

Remember to Explain Your Answer

Would you rather be the person that discovered the Easter Islands OR be the first person to meet the Easter Bunny?

Funny Point____/1

Would you rather discover a new, exotic flower that only grows in spring OR have someone else discover it and name it after you?

Funny Point____/1

🥕 Easter Egg 1

_____/6

Round 4 Total Score

🥕 Easter Egg 2

_____/6

Round 4 Total Score

ROUND

5

Easter Egg 1

Remember to Explain Your Answer

Would you rather smell like fresh flowers OR smell like chocolate for your whole life?

Funny Point____/1

Would you rather be forced to stop and smell every flower you pass by OR be forced to eat every piece of chocolate you see even if you're full or if it's someone else's chocolate?

Funny Point____/1

Easter Egg 1

Remember to Explain Your Answer

Would you rather the whole of spring be too hot OR the whole of summer be too cold?

Funny Point____/1

Would you rather have a spring vacation anywhere in the world you want OR have a winter vacation anywhere in the world you want?

Funny Point____/1

Easter Egg 1

Remember to Explain Your Answer

Would you rather have your room be filled from the floor to the ceiling with spring flowers OR have your whole house be filled with bugs?

Funny Point____/1

Would you rather search for Easter eggs outside when it's so hot you can fry an egg on the road OR search for Easter eggs inside your house but you'll only find half as many eggs as you would find if you were searching outside?

Funny Point____/1

STOP: Now pass the book to Easter Egg 2

Easter Egg 1

Remember to Explain Your Answer

Id you rather have your room be
d from the floor to the ceiling
h spring flowers OR have your
ole house be filled with bugs?

Funny Point____/1

d you rather search for Easter eggs
le when it's so hot you can fry an egg
he road OR search for Easter eggs
ide your house but you'll only find
lf as many eggs as you would find
if you were searching outside?

Funny Point____/1

STOP: Now pass the book to Easter Egg 2

ROUND

5

Would you rather smell like fresh flowers OR smell like chocolate for your whole life?

Funny Point____/1

Would you rather be forced to stop and smell every flower you pass by OR be forced to eat every piece of chocolate you see even if you're full or if it's someone else's chocolate?

Funny Point____/1

42

Easter E

Remember to Explain Yo

Would you rather the w be too hot OR the summer be too

Funr

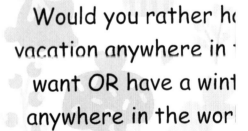

Would you rather he vacation anywhere in want OR have a wint anywhere in the wor

Funi

43

Wou
fill
wit
wh

Wou
outsi
on t
ins
hc

Easter Egg 2

Remember to Explain Your Answer

Would you rather have to turn into a talking flower OR have to turn into an egg for the whole of spring?

Funny Point____/1

Would you rather eat fried chocolate eggs and jellybean flavored toast for breakfast OR eat tiny hot-cross buns in a bowl of milk?

Funny Point____/1

Easter Egg 2

Remember to Explain Your Answer

Would you rather go stargazing or learn how to make a rabbit crochet?

Funny Point____/1

Would you rather live on the Easter Islands all alone and it be Easter every day OR live in a town where you have lots of friends but nobody in the town celebrates Easter?

Funny Point____/1

Easter Egg 2

Remember to Explain Your Answer

Would you rather eat only carrots
OR plant carrots for a month?

Funny Point____/1

Would you rather poop jellybeans like
the Easter Bunny OR poop cupcakes
like a magical Unicorn?

Funny Point____/1

 # Easter Egg 1

_____/6

Round 5 Total Score

Easter Egg 2

_____/6

Round 5 Total Score

ROUND

6

Easter Egg 1

Remember to Explain Your Answer

Would you rather have pointy ears like a bunny OR yellow feathers like a baby chick?

Funny Point____/1

Would you rather live in a house made of chocolate OR a house made of jellybeans?

Funny Point____/1

50

Easter Egg 1

Remember to Explain Your Answer

Would you rather learn how to make ice cream OR learn how to make rainbow cupcakes?

Funny Point____/1

Would you rather participate in an egg and spoon race OR a three-legged race?

Funny Point____/1

Easter Egg 1

Remember to Explain Your Answer

Would you rather learn how to catch a leprechaun OR the Easter Bunny?

Funny Point____/1

Would you rather have a magic burrow that can lead you to anywhere you want to go or have Santa's magic sleigh with all the reindeers?

Funny Point____/1

STOP: Now pass the book to Easter Egg 2

Easter Egg 2

Remember to Explain Your Answer

Would you rather know the names of every single flower in the world OR know every rabbit species in the world?

Funny Point____/1

Would you rather have dinner at a restaurant where all the waiters are bunnies OR be waiter/waitress in a restaurant that only serve bunnies?

Funny Point____/1

Easter Egg 2

Remember to Explain Your Answer

Would you rather only drink carrot juice OR eat only marshmallows for the entire Easter day?

Funny Point____/1

Would you rather make Easter cards OR make Easter gift baskets for all your classmates?

Funny Point____/1

Easter Egg 2

Remember to Explain Your Answer

Would you rather have your mom be the Easter Bunny OR your older sibling as the Easter Bunny?

Funny Point____/1

Would you rather be given a live bunny for Easter OR a live reindeer for Christmas?

Funny Point____/1

Easter Egg 1

_____/6

Round 6 Total Score

Easter Egg 2

_____/6

Round 6 Total Score

ROUND

7

Easter Egg 1

Remember to Explain Your Answer

Would you rather live in a house
with 100 rabbits OR live in a house
with 100 baby chicks?

Funny Point____/1

Would you rather wear a coat made
out of jellybeans OR a coat made out
of Easter eggs?

Funny Point____/1

Easter Egg 1

Remember to Explain Your Answer

Would you rather have breakfast with the Easter Bunny OR with Santa Claus?

Funny Point____/1

Would you rather have Iron Man OR the Hulk dressed up as the Easter Bunny and go egg hunting with you?

Funny Point____/1

Easter Egg 1

Remember to Explain Your Answer

Would you rather have to catch flying Easter eggs with a net OR have to dig for them under the ground?

Funny Point____/1

Would you rather be able to talk to bunnies OR be able to talk to all other animals?

Funny Point____/1

STOP: Now pass the book to Easter Egg 2

60

Easter Egg 2

Remember to Explain Your Answer

Would you rather fly to the moon in an Easter egg shaped rocket OR Easter Bunny shaped rocket?

Funny Point____/1

Would you rather eat only raw carrots OR chocolate covered carrots on Easter day?

Funny Point____/1

Easter Egg 2

Would you rather it rain on Easter day OR it snow on Easter day?

Funny Point____/1

Would you rather live in a burrow with the Easter Bunny OR in a castle made of fluffy white clouds?

Funny Point____/1

62

Easter Egg 2

Remember to Explain Your Answer

Would you rather be the child of the Easter Bunny or the sibling of a leprechaun?

Funny Point____/1

Would you rather find a pot of gold at the end of the rainbow OR 100 Easter eggs?

Funny Point____/1

🥕 Easter Egg 1

_____/6

Round 7 Total Score

🥕 Easter Egg 2

_____/6

Round 7 Total Score

ROUND

8

Easter Egg 1

Remember to Explain Your Answer

Would you rather have a bunny robot as your personal assistant or you be the personal assistant to the Easter Bunny?

Funny Point____/1

Would you rather be terrible at singing and participate in an Easter musical or be great at singing and not participate in any musical?

Funny Point____/1

Easter Egg 1

Remember to Explain Your Answer

Would you rather visit Disney World on Easter day or on Christmas day?

Funny Point____/1

Would you rather have no teeth or have teeth made of jellybeans?

Funny Point____/1

Easter Egg 1

Remember to Explain Your Answer

Would you rather have a rabbit genie that will grant you a wish after you eat 10 carrots OR have a rabbit fairy godmother will protect you but not grant you any wishes?

Funny Point____/1

Would you rather eat chocolate beef stew OR chocolate covered barbeque ribs?

Funny Point____/1

STOP: Now pass the book to Easter Egg 2

Easter Egg 2

Remember to Explain Your Answer

Would you rather hatch a chick from an Easter Egg and keep it as a pet OR hatch a dinosaur from a dinosaur egg and keep it as a pet?

Funny Point____/1

Would you rather have bunny whiskers OR a fluffy cotton bunny tail ?

Funny Point____/1

Easter Egg 2

Remember to Explain Your Answer

Would you rather be able to talk to butterflies OR have a bunny constantly hopping in a circle around you ?

Funny Point____/1

Would you rather learn how to harvest honey from a beehive OR learn how to make gummy bears?

Funny Point____/1

Remember to Explain Your Answer

Would you rather give your friends giant chocolate Easter eggs OR small plastic Easter eggs with $5 inside?

Funny Point____/1

Would you rather paint Easter eggs OR learn how to shape a bunny using chocolate?

Funny Point____/1

Easter Egg 1

_____/6

Round 8 Total Score

Easter Egg 2

_____/6

Round 8 Total Score

ROUND 9

Easter Egg 1

Remember to Explain Your Answer

Would you rather go on an underwater Easter egg hunt OR on an Easter egg hunt in the jungle?

Funny Point____/1

Would you rather have the Easter egg you find be made out of gold OR diamonds?

Funny Point____/1

Easter Egg 1

Remember to Explain Your Answer

Would you rather have all the vegetables you eat taste like chocolate OR all the chocolate you eat to taste like vegetables ?

Funny Point____/1

Would you rather have to sing a song about baby bunnies OR recite a poem about Easter eggs in front of your entire school?

Funny Point____/1

Easter Egg 1

Remember to Explain Your Answer

Would you rather have to paint 250 Easter eggs OR find 500 jellybeans in the backyard?

Funny Point____/1

Would you rather have a secret identity as the Easter Bunny OR Santa Claus?

Funny Point____/1

STOP: Now pass the book to Easter Egg 2

Easter Egg 2

Remember to Explain Your Answer

Would you rather have to tuck 3 baby bunnies OR tuck 10 puppies one by one to sleep?

Funny Point____/1

Would you rather have to eat Easter dinner prepared by your pet dog or eat a big bowl of mayonaise?

Funny Point____/1

Easter Egg 2

Remember to Explain Your Answer

Would you rather have flowers grow on anything you touched OR be able to turn anything into cotton candy?

Funny Point____/1

Would you rather be able to blow confetti or bubbles out of your mouth?

Funny Point____/1

Easter Egg 2

Remember to Explain Your Answer

Would you rather have to unwrap 500 pieces of foiled wrapped chocolate bunnies or eat 500 small chocolate Easter eggs ?

Funny Point____/1

Would you rather drink a glass of rotten carrot chocolate smoothie or eat a piece of chocolate covered grasshopper?

Funny Point____/1

Easter Egg 1

_____/6
Round 9 Total Score

Easter Egg 2

_____/6
Round 9 Total Score

ROUND

10

Easter Egg 1

Would you rather be allergic to bunnies OR allergic to chocolate?

Funny Point____/1

Would you rather learn how to say Happy Easter in 100 different languages OR taste chocolates from 100 different countries?

Funny Point____/1

Easter Egg 1

Remember to Explain Your Answer

Would you rather have a pet rabbit that poops out chocolate OR have a pet frog that is made of chocolate?

Funny Point____/1

Would you rather be able to hop really high like a kangaroo OR be able to hop really fast like a bunny??

Funny Point____/1

Easter Egg 1

Remember to Explain Your Answer

Would you rather have the ability to make flowers grow really fast and big OR have the ability to make a wish every time you plant a tree?

Funny Point____/1

Would you rather take a swim in a pool filled with melted chocolate OR swim in a pool filled with cake batter?

Funny Point____/1

STOP: Now pass the book to Easter Egg 2

Easter Egg 2

Remember to Explain Your Answer

Would you rather travel to Easter Island on a magic flying carpet OR in bunny shaped spaceship?

Funny Point____/1

Would you rather stay up late on the night before Easter and wake up late to search for eggs or go to bed early and wake up early to search for eggs?

Funny Point____/1

Easter Egg 2

Remember to Explain Your Answer

Would you rather only be able to taste jellybeans and not be able to taste anything else or be able to taste everything except chocolate?

Funny Point____/1

Would you rather be the star in a movie about Easter OR write a song about Easter?

Funny Point____/1

Easter Egg 2

Remember to Explain Your Answer

Would you rather only be able to eat bitter chocolate OR spicy chocolate for the rest of your life?

Funny Point____/1

Would you rather have Aquaman help you look for your Easter eggs OR have Wonder Woman hide your Easter eggs?

Funny Point____/1

 Easter Egg 1

_____/6

Round 10 Total Score

Easter Egg 2

_____/6

Round 10 Total Score

ROUND
II

Tie Breaker

Add up each player's score from all previous rounds. If the points result in a Tie, move on to the Tie Breaker round

Easter Egg 1 _____/10
Grand Total

Easter Egg 2 _____/10
Grand Total

Easter Egg 1

Would you rather have to carry a dozen of raw eggs OR carry 50 plastic eggs with you wherever you go for an whole month?

Funny Point____/1

Would you rather be able to hop like a frog and smell like a bunny OR hop like a bunny and smell like a frog?

Funny Point____/1

Easter Egg 1

Remember to Explain Your Answer

Would you rather have a large, plastic-egg-shaped body OR have plastic green grass for hair?

Funny Point____/1

Would you rather have a jellybean stuck in your teeth for an entire week or wear a half melted chocolate hat?

Funny Point____/1

Easter Egg 1

Would you rather eat an entire 4lb chocolate bunny or 4lbs of jellybeans?

Funny Point____/1

Would you rather be the captain of a group of pirate bunnies or the leader of a group of crime fighting super bunnies?

Funny Point____/1

STOP: Now pass the book to Easter Egg 2

Easter Egg 2

Remember to Explain Your Answer

Would you rather cook the entire Easter meal using only carrots or chocolates?

Funny Point____/1

Would you rather celebrate Easter with no electricity or no candy?

Funny Point____/1

Would you rather have to sneeze every time someone wishes you Happy Easter OR have hiccups for the entire Easter day ?

Funny Point____/1

Would you rather walk around with a chocolate mustache or a milk mustache ?

Funny Point____/1

Easter Egg 2

Remember to Explain Your Answer

Would you rather eat a dozen Easter chocolate eggs or a dozen of marshmallow at one time?

Funny Point____/1

Would you rather kiss a toad and get as many chocolate you want OR hold a porcupine as you look for Easter eggs?

Funny Point____/1

Easter Egg 1

_____/6

Round 11 Total Score

Easter Egg 2

_____/6

Round 11 Total Score

_____

The Ultimate
Kids Laugh Challenge
Master

Did you enjoy the book?

If you did, we are ecstatic. If not, please write your complaint to us and we will make sure to fix it.

If you're feeling generous, there is something important that you can help me with – tell other people that you enjoyed the book.

Ask a grown-up to write about it on Amazon. When they do, more people will find out about the book. It also lets Amazon know that we are making kids around the world laugh. Even a few words and ratings would go a long way.

If you have any ideas or jokes that you think are super funny, please let us know. We would love to hear from you. Our email address is - **joylandforkids@gmail.com**

About Joyland

Joyland is a mom + dad run publishing company. We are passionate about creating fun and innovative books to help children develop their reading skills and fall in love with reading. If you have suggestions for us or want to work with us, shoot us an email at **joylandforkids@gmail.com**

Our favourite family quote

"The activities that are the easiest, cheapest, and most fun to do – such as singing, playing games, reading, storytelling, and just talking and listening – are also the best for child development."
~ Jerome Singer

Made in the USA
Columbia, SC
01 April 2020

90306924R00054